MW01228038

PRAYING
GOD'S WORD
-For Teens and Young Adults-

by STEPHANIE A. MAYBERRY

Presented to

Presented by

Date

PRAYING
GOD'S WORD
-For Teens and Young Adults-

STEPHANIE A. MAYBERRY

All scriptures used in this text are taken from the
New American Standard Bible.

STEPHANIE A. MAYBERRY

Copyright © 2012 Stephanie A. Mayberry

ISBN-10: 1475134401
ISBN-13: 978-1475134407

Printed in the U.S.A.

:

BOOKS BY STEPHANIE A. MAYBERRY

My Testimony

101 Simple ways to Minister to Others

7 Steps to a Godly Marriage

Praying God's Word: For Teens and Young Adults

HEALING FOR THE BATTERED SPIRIT SERIES

My Story is not Unique (a story about domestic violence)

Why I Stayed: Ministering to the Battered Spirit

More Valuable than Sparrows: Healing for the Battered Spirit

Ministering to the Battered Spirit: A Ministry Kit for Battling the Spirit of Abuse

THE CHRISTIAN ASPIE SERIES

Fringe: My Life as a Spirit-Filled Christian with Asperger's Syndrome

More Fringe: My Growth as a Spirit-Filled Christian with Asperger's Syndrome

Deeper Fringe: My Joy as a Spirit-Filled Christian with Asperger's Syndrome (coming soon!)

The Christian Aspie: Notes from the Blog

STEPHANIE A. MAYBERRY

DEDICATION

I dedicate this book to all who want a closer, more personal, more intimate relationship with Jesus. He is life, He is light, He is love and the closer you walk with Him, the more like Him you will be. The road will not always be easy, but the rewards are so great!

Praise Jesus!.

STEPHANIE A. MAYBERRY

Dear Reader,

If the words in my books speak to you, resonate with you, touch you, please know it isn't really me, it is God speaking to you.

See, I am just a vessel that He uses to convey His message to you, to others. I am no great writer; I am just the obedient hand that holds the pen for the greatest author of all – my God.

He alone deserves all of the praise, all the glory.

Thank you so much for your support and encouragement. Each and every email, every word, every letter is such a treasure to me! I pray for your continued growth in your relationship with God. Forever walk in His Word and you will know blessings beyond your imagination.

God is so good, isn't He?

Stephanie Mayberry

STEPHANIE A. MAYBERRY

.

CONTENTS

ACKNOWLEDGMENTS

I could not do this without God's gentle, guiding hand. With each book I write, He reveals more of His Truth to me. As I am writing, I am learning. This isn't an accident, or chance or luck or even education, but it is a direct communion with the Holy Spirit. It is living in the Spirit and walking in the Word, doing the very best that I can to live for God and make my life a living example of Godly living. I am not always successful in this and I thank God every day that He is a forgiving God who loves me despite my humanness. Above all, I acknowledge Him for without His guidance, this would be nothing more than mere words on a page. Instead, it is something far greater and more important – and He has allowed me the privilege of communicating it to you..

STEPHANIE A. MAYBERRY

1

PRAYING GOD'S WORD

It's a tough world out there! Young people are faced with many more stressors and temptations than their parents were. In an age where "sex sells" and a media that glorifies sin is saturating our society, it is more important than ever to protect yourself. It is time to take up that mighty sword of God's Word and fight those things that hell is throwing at you!

> [17] And take THE HELMET OF SALVATION, and the sword of the Spirit, which is the word of God. ~Ephesians 6:17

God's Word, that mighty sword, will show you the righteous path, guide you in your daily life and show you what to pray when the world seems out of control and life seems full of difficulties. Praying God's Word is a powerful weapon against hell because you are praying His own Words back to Him.

> [16] All Scripture is inspired by God and profitable for teaching, for reproof, for correction, for training in righteousness; [17] so that the man of God may be adequate, equipped for every good work. ~2 Timothy 3:16-17

What happens when you pray God's Word is that not only are you praying His Words back to Him, but you are also infusing His Word in your spirit. It will become a part of you. When you pray His Word in earnestness and with a contrite heart you will touch God. You will get results.

Jesus said, "It is the Spirit who gives life; the flesh profits nothing; the words that I have spoken to you are spirit and are life." (John 6:63).

Paul had this to say about God's Word:

> For the word of God is living and active and sharper than any two-edged sword, and piercing as far as the division of soul and spirit, of both joints and marrow, and able to judge the thoughts and intentions of the heart. ~Hebrews 4:12

So, if you are praying God's Word, you are praying life and spirit and truth and power. You are placing His Word into your spirit so that you speak it, pray it and live it. You are wielding a mighty weapon against hell and the temptations of this world.

But even the mightiest weapon is useless if you don't know how to use it properly.

When you are praying God's Word, you must speak it aloud. At least speak the words loud enough for you to hear yourself. When God created the world, He **spoke** it into creation. Throughout the Bible, you will see an emphasis on speaking, on controlling the tongue.

Solomon did not mince words when he said, "Death and life are in the power of the tongue, and those who love it will eat its fruit." (Proverbs 18:21)

James warned us, "If anyone thinks himself to be religious, and yet does not bridle his tongue but deceives his own heart, this man's religion is worthless." (James 1:26)

The tongue is the most unruly part of a person's body and when you can bring it under submission to God you can attain a spiritual depth that is more fulfilling and richer than you thought possible. That is why it is so important to pray aloud, read your Bible aloud and Pray God's Word aloud. When you do that, you change the atmosphere around you and it changes you.

You will notice that this book is broken down into sections. Each section addresses specific issues and challenges that you may face. This isn't necessarily a book that you read from cover to cover; rather you read and pray the section that is relevant to your situation.

Some sections, such as "Praying God's Word for your Spiritual Growth" and "Praying God's Word in Praise," are things you can and should be praying every single day. The deeper you get into God and His Word, the more you will find yourself seeking Him through prayer and His Word.

And the better equipped you are to handle the difficulties of life.

I have selected a few verses for each section, but by all means explore your Bible for more! God has so many wonderful things He wants to show you, wants you to know through His Word! If I included every single applicable scripture for each section this book would be overwhelming. So, I prayed over it for a few days and then chose only a few. But I encourage further study. God wants you to look further and dig deeper. And as I write these words, I feel a powerful move of the Holy Spirit. This is just a taste of what He has for you, the power that lies within your Bible. This is only a beginning point.

So, keep it up! Set aside a time every single day to meet with God, to pray and to immerse yourself in His Word. Start small if you must, but always seek to grow and get deeper into Him. It is absolutely vital that you spend time with God, praying and reading the Bible every single day. This book is a good place to start, but don't let it end here.

2

HOW TO USE THIS BOOK

This little book should be used every day.

You will see that it is divided into several sections. Each section addresses a specific issue or area of prayer.

Each section has several verses that directly relate to that area. Some, like many of the Psalms, can be read as a prayer. Others, however, provide direction and guidance for what to pray for and what to strive to attain. In those cases, you will see a verse or set of verses with a prayer below it. Read those verses, and then pray that prayer.

It is important that when to go to a section you read it in its entirety. Each section is set up in a specific way so start at the beginning of the section and pray your way through it entirely. Speak the words aloud, do not be silent! These words carry power and life and light, they must be released into the atmosphere, into the world.

As you pray, think about the verses, let them sink in. Once you finish the section, you may feel led to pray more. You can certainly pray that section again, or you can just pray what is on your heart, what comes from those verses.

While you will have the guided prayers to follow along with the scripture, it is vitally important that you read the Word for yourself, ingest it and let God guide you on how you should pray on the things in your life.

The more you do it, the more natural it will become. And the more you will be honoring God.

I can't stress enough how important it is to have a prayer life. Your relationship with God depends on it!

My daughter and I are prayer buddies. She lives in another state, but every night at a certain time we text each other and pray. We started at 10 minutes, but we always seem to go longer. Being prayer buddies, though, makes each of us accountable. We share prayer requests and connect before and after. It has become a part of our day that we both look forward to and God is honoring it in wonderful ways.

The only way to have a mind of Christ (1 Corinthians 2:16) is to meet with Him in prayer every day, preferably at the same time each day. Just start out 10 minutes at a time, at the same time every day. If you submit to Him and pour yourself into your prayer I promise you that your walk with Him will be closer and deeper – and you'll forget about that time limit! He rewards faithfulness and obedience.

Praying God's Word

for your Spiritual Growth

[8] The LORD will accomplish what concerns me;
Your loving kindness, O LORD, is everlasting;
Do not forsake the works of Your hands. **~Psalm 138:8**

[6] For I am confident of this very thing, that He who began a good work in you will perfect it until the day of Christ **~Philippians 1:6**

[22] But the fruit of the Spirit is love, joy, peace, patience, kindness, goodness, faithfulness, [23] gentleness, self-control; against such things there is no law. **~Galatians 5:22-23**

[6] Therefore as you have received Christ Jesus the Lord, so walk in Him, [7] having been firmly rooted and now being built up in Him and established in your faith, just as you were instructed, and overflowing with gratitude. **~Colossians 2:6-7**

Jesus, I want you to live in me so that Your light shines from me and Your fruits are mine. Lord, help me to bring these things into my life: love, joy, peace, patience, kindness, goodness, faithfulness, gentleness and self-control. Perfect that good work you began in me. I want to walk in you, be firmly rooted in you and be built up in you. Live in me, Jesus and I will always give you the glory.

[23] Search me, O God, and know my heart;
Try me and know my anxious thoughts;
[24] And see if there be any hurtful way in me,

And lead me in the everlasting way. **~Psalm 139:23-24**

[1] O LORD, You have searched me and known me.
[2] You know when I sit down and when I rise up;
You understand my thought from afar.
[3] You scrutinize my path and my lying down,
And are intimately acquainted with all my ways.
[4] Even before there is a word on my tongue,
Behold, O LORD, You know it all. **~Psalm 139:1-4**

[10] Create in me a clean heart, O God,
And renew a steadfast spirit within me.
[11] Do not cast me away from Your presence
And do not take Your Holy Spirit from me.
[12] Restore to me the joy of Your salvation
And sustain me with a willing spirit. **~Psalm 51:10-12**

[4] Make me know Your ways, O LORD;
Teach me Your paths.
[5] Lead me in Your truth and teach me,
For You are the God of my salvation;
For You I wait all the day.
[6] Remember, O LORD, Your compassion and Your lovingkindnesses,
For they have been from of old.
[7] Do not remember the sins of my youth or my transgressions;
According to Your lovingkindness remember me,
For Your goodness' sake, O LORD. **~Psalm 25:4-7**

Praying God's Word

for your Family

1 Children, obey your parents in the Lord, for this is right.
~Ephesians 6:1

[8] Hear, my son, your father's instruction And do not forsake your mother's teaching; **~Proverbs 1:8**

[5] and you have forgotten the exhortation which is addressed to you as sons,

"MY SON, DO NOT REGARD LIGHTLY THE DISCIPLINE OF THE LORD, NOR FAINT WHEN YOU ARE REPROVED BY HIM; [6] FOR THOSE WHOM THE LORD LOVES HE DISCIPLINES, AND HE SCOURGES EVERY SON WHOM HE RECEIVES."

[7] It is for discipline that you endure; God deals with you as with sons; for what son is there whom *his* father does not discipline? [8] But if you are without discipline, of which all have become partakers, then you are illegitimate children and not sons. **~Hebrews 12:5-8**

[4] Fathers, do not provoke your children to anger, but bring them up in the discipline and instruction of the Lord.
~ Ephesians 6:4

[6] These words, which I am commanding you today, shall be on your heart. [7] You shall teach them diligently to your sons and shall talk of them when you sit in your house and when you walk by the way and when you lie down and when you rise up. **~Deuteronomy 6:6-7**

[33] But seek first His kingdom and His righteousness, and all these things will be added to you. ~**Matthew 6:33**

Lord, please place your hedge of protection around my family. Help me to be the child you said I should be, that I obey my parents and hear their instruction, that I not forsake their teaching. (Pray this for siblings as well)

Make my parents strong, Lord, help them stay strong in You so that they are good examples to me and help me to grow in you. Give them wisdom in their discipline and instruction and let discipline come from love not anger.

I pray for my parents, Jesus. Make them strong in Your Word. Give my father wisdom and strength in leading our family as you have appointed him. Give my parents a heart for you and make their paths straight so that I can follow their example.

Lord, keep my family safe and guide us in all that we do. Help us to love and respect each other, forming close and loving relationships.

I thank You, Jesus, for my family.

Praying God's Word

for your Unsaved Family Members and Friends

¹⁴ This is the confidence which we have before Him, that, if we ask anything according to His will, He hears us. ¹⁵ And if we know that He hears us in whatever we ask, we know that we have the requests which we have asked from Him.
~1 John 5:14-15

⁹ The Lord is not slow about His promise, as some count slowness, but is patient toward you, not wishing for any to perish but for all to come to repentance. **~2 Peter 3:9**

⁵⁶ for the Son of Man did not come to destroy men's lives, but to save them…**~Luke 9:56**

¹⁹ "God is not a man, that He should lie,
Nor a son of man, that He should repent;
Has He said, and will He not do it?
Or has He spoken, and will He not make it good?
~Numbers 23:19

³³ "But this is the covenant which I will make with the house of Israel after those days," declares the LORD, "I will put My law within them and on their heart I will write it; and I will be their God, and they shall be My people.
~Jeremiah 31:33

Lord, You said that anything I ask that is according to Your will, You will hear. You have come to save souls and it is Your will that [speak the name of the friend/parent/loved one] should not perish, but that they would come to repentance. Your Word says that

You cannot lie. Please, Lord, save them! I speak in faith that you will deliver my loved one, that you will give them a heart that is hungry for You, that seeks You, that You will put Your law within them and write it on their heart so that they will be Yours and You will be their God.

Praying God's Word

for the God Appointed Authority in your Life

STEPHANIE A. MAYBERRY

Parents

[12] "Honor your father and your mother, that your days may be prolonged in the land which the LORD your God gives you. ~**Exodus 20:12**

[8] Hear, my son, your father's instruction
And do not forsake your mother's teaching; ~**Proverbs 1:8**

Lord, give me a heart to honor my father and my mother, teach me how to be obedient, learning from them and keeping them in the place you have appointed them in my life. Guide them to lead with integrity and compassion and obedience to you, to hunger for you and to walk in Your Word. Lord, help me to know that they will fall, but strike the root of bitterness from me so that it cannot take hold of me that I may continue to respect, love and honor them as You command. And raise them when they fall; receive their repentance with loving, open arms.

Government

[1] First of all, then, I urge that entreaties and prayers, petitions and thanksgivings, be made on behalf of all men, [2] for kings and all who are in authority, so that we may lead a tranquil and quiet life in all godliness and dignity. ~**1 Timothy 2:1-2**

Jesus, I give thanks for our government. Lift up those in authority over us, imparting wisdom and compassion and a heart for You. Move through our government, seeking out your saints, binding us together so that we present an insurmountable force against the enemy, carrying Your spirit through every hall, into every office, touching every heart and mind. Pour out Your spirit onto them and make Your Word known to them. Cause them to be men and women of integrity and obedient to Your Word for us. Open their ears to Godly counsel and soften their hearts so that they may receive it. Let Your power and glory move through this place, Lord, easing burdens and bringing peace to troubled hearts and minds. Silence the enemy, binding him in Jesus' precious name so that he may no longer operate against us, against our country, against our government, against our leaders.

All Authorities (including bosses, teachers, etc.)

[23] Whatever you do, do your work heartily, as for the Lord rather than for men, **~Colossians 3:23**

Lord, please help me to remember that all authority in my life is appointed by you and that by honoring those placed over me I am honoring you. Help me to keep a right attitude and to work as if I am working for you.

[1] Every person is to be in subjection to the governing authorities. For there is no authority except from God, and those which exist are established by God. [2] Therefore whoever resists authority has opposed the ordinance of God; and they who have opposed will receive condemnation upon themselves. [3] For rulers are not a cause of fear for good behavior, but for evil. Do you want to have no fear of authority? Do what is good and you will have praise from the same; [4] for it is a minister of God to you for good. But if you do what is evil, be afraid; for it does not bear the sword for nothing; for it is a minister of God, an avenger who brings wrath on the one who practices evil. [5] Therefore it is necessary to be in subjection, not only because of wrath, but also for conscience' sake.
~Romans 13:1-5

Lord, help me to keep a right attitude about the God appointed authority in my life. Put leadership in my life that is Godly and fair and of good character. But help me to remember that even authority that is evil is still appointed over me by You and that I should still do good and do what is right, being obedient unless it directs me to break your laws. Teach me how to honor you through my work and through my honor of the God appointed authority in my life.

Praying God's Word

against Peer Pressure

STEPHANIE A. MAYBERRY

[18] For I know that nothing good dwells in me, that is, in my flesh; for the willing is present in me, but the doing of the good is not. [19] For the good that I want, I do not do, but I practice the very evil that I do not want.
~Romans 7:18-19

[2] And do not be conformed to this world, but be transformed by the renewing of your mind, so that you may prove what the will of God is, that which is good and acceptable and perfect. **~Romans 12:2**

[14] But put on the Lord Jesus Christ, and make no provision for the flesh in regard to its lusts. **~Romans 13:14**

[20] I have been crucified with Christ; and it is no longer I who live, but Christ lives in me; and the life which I now live in the flesh I live by faith in the Son of God, who loved me and gave Himself up for me. **~Galatians 2:20**

Jesus, I want to do right, I really do, but sometimes it just seems easier to go along with what everyone else does. Give me wisdom and strength to deal with peer pressure when it is presented to me. Open my eyes so that I can recognize it and give me the courage to resist what I know is wrong. Give me the words to cast it away so that I am not swayed by it.

Let my actions influence others to resist peer pressure and to turn to You when they are tempted so that they too will be strong to stand for You.

Let my life, my words, my actions reflect you and give you glory. Keep me pure and keep me safe from the influences of the world. Set me apart; do not let me be conformed to this world. Transform me, renew my mind so that I reflect you and what is good and acceptable and perfect.

Live in me, Jesus, let me put you on and cast away the ways of the world, live in me so that I may live by Your Word and know your love and acceptance, understanding that that is all I need.

[4] Keep me, O LORD, from the hands of the wicked;
Preserve me from violent men
Who have purposed to trip up my feet.
[5] The proud have hidden a trap for me, and cords;
They have spread a net by the wayside;
They have set snares for me. **~Psalm 140:4-5**

Praying God's Word

for Moral Purity

[29] …We must obey God rather than men. **~Acts 5:29**

[15] If you love Me, you will keep My commandments. **~John 14:15**

[11] Beloved, I urge you as aliens and strangers to abstain from fleshly lusts which wage war against the soul. **~ 1 Peter 2:11**

[33] Do not be deceived: "Bad company corrupts good morals." **~1 Corinthians 15:33**

[9] Or do you not know that the unrighteous will not inherit the kingdom of God? Do not be deceived; neither fornicators, nor idolaters, nor adulterers, nor effeminate, nor homosexuals, [10] nor thieves, nor *the* covetous, nor drunkards, nor revilers, nor swindlers, will inherit the kingdom of God.. **~1 Corinthians 6:9-10**

[22] But prove yourselves doers of the word, and not merely hearers who delude themselves. **~James 1:22**

[13] Therefore, prepare your minds for action, keep sober *in spirit*, fix your hope completely on the grace to be brought to you at the revelation of Jesus Christ. **[14]** As obedient children, do not be conformed to the former lusts *which were yours* in your ignorance, **[15]** but like the Holy One who called you, be holy yourselves also in all *your* behavior; **[16]** because it is written, "YOU SHALL BE HOLY, FOR I AM HOLY." **~1 Peter 1:13-16**

[22] Now flee from youthful lusts and pursue righteousness, faith, love *ana* peace, with those who call on the Lord from a pure heart. **~2 Timothy 2:22**

Lord, I do love you and I want to keep your commandments, I want to obey you, not men, not the world, but sometimes that is not an easy thing to do! Please help me abstain from lusts of the flesh. Keep my eyes open so that I am not swayed by bad company. Help me to choose my friends wisely.

I want to inherit your kingdom, Lord, please make me wise to the lies of the enemy so that I do not fall into any of his traps. Help me to not only hear Your Word, but to do it, to put it into action, to live it. Help me to walk in Your Word every single day.

Help me to keep my eyes on You, my mind on You and not be conformed to the world and a slave to my flesh. Help me to flee from my youthful lusts and pursue instead what is pure and righteous; pursue faith, love and peace. Live in me, Lord, so I can be like You.

Praying God's Word

to Control your Tongue

STEPHANIE A. MAYBERRY

²¹ Death and life are in the power of the tongue,
And those who love it will eat its fruit. **~Proverbs 18:21**

³⁴ You brood of vipers, how can you, being evil, speak what is good? For the mouth speaks out of that which fills the heart. ³⁵ The good man brings out of his good treasure what is good; and the evil man brings out of his evil treasure what is evil. ³⁶ But I tell you that every careless word that people speak, they shall give an accounting for it in the Day of Judgment. ³⁷ For by your words you will be justified, and by your words you will be condemned."
~Matthew 12:34-37

¹⁹ This you know, my beloved brethren. But everyone must be quick to hear, slow to speak and slow to anger
~James 1:19

Lord, Your Word says that the power of life and death lies in the tongue. It says that my mouth will speak what is in my heart. Help me to tame my tongue. I want to bring out good treasure and not speak careless words.

Help me to keep from all manner of evil speaking so that I do not curse or complain or argue or blaspheme or lie or speak against my brothers and sisters. Help me to be slow to speak and quick to hear.

Let the things that come from my mouth glorify You and show Your spirit living within me.

⁴ My lips certainly will not speak unjustly,
Nor will my tongue mutter deceit. **~Job 27:4**

¹ "I will guard my ways
That I may not sin with my tongue;
I will guard my mouth as with a muzzle
While the wicked are in my presence." **~Psalm 39:1**

Praying God's Word

against Drugs and Alcohol

¹⁹ Or do you not know that your body is a temple of the Holy Spirit who is in you, whom you have from God, and that you are not your own? **~1 Corinthians 6:19**

Lord, my body is your temple; it is not mine, but Yours. Please help me to treat it as a holy place and help me to resist temptation.

¹⁹ Now the deeds of the flesh are evident, which are: immorality, impurity, sensuality, ²⁰ idolatry, sorcery, enmities, strife, jealousy, outbursts of anger, disputes, dissensions, factions, ²¹ envying, drunkenness, carousing, and things like these, of which I forewarn you, just as I have forewarned you, that those who practice such things will not inherit the kingdom of God. **~Galatians 5:19-21**

¹ Wine is a mocker, strong drink a brawler,
And whoever is intoxicated by it is not wise.
~Proverbs 20:1

⁸ Be of sober *spirit*, be on the alert. Your adversary, the devil, prowls around like a roaring lion, seeking someone to devour. **~1 Peter 5:8**

Jesus, I want to inherit your kingdom! I want to be wise and alert, but I know that putting drugs and alcohol into my body make me unwise and sluggish, leaving me an easy target for the enemy to attack and devour. Help me to keep my mind sharp and treat my body as Your holy temple so that the enemy cannot get a foothold in my life.

[21] But examine everything carefully; hold fast to that which is good; [22] abstain from every form of evil.
~1 Thessalonians 5:22

[5] Therefore consider the members of your earthly body as dead to immorality, impurity, passion, evil desire, and greed, which amounts to idolatry. **~Colossians 3:5**

Lord, kill off the things in me that offend You, that do not please You and fill me with You. Make me wise so that I can examine everything carefully and recognize evil. Make me strong so that I can resist it no matter what everyone else is doing.

Praying God's Word

against Stress and Worry

²⁷ And who of you by being worried can add a single hour to his life? ²⁸ And why are you worried about clothing? Observe how the lilies of the field grow; they do not toil nor do they spin, ²⁹ yet I say to you that not even Solomon in all his glory clothed himself like one of these. ³⁰ But if God so clothes the grass of the field, which is alive today and tomorrow is thrown into the furnace, will He not much more clothe you? You of little faith! **~Matthew 6:27-30**

²⁵ Anxiety in a man's heart weighs it down,
But a good word makes it glad. **~Proverbs 12:25**

⁶ Be anxious for nothing, but in everything by prayer and supplication with thanksgiving let your requests be made known to God. ⁷ And the peace of God, which surpasses all comprehension, will guard your hearts and your minds in Christ Jesus. **~Philippians 4:6-7**

³¹ Do not worry then, saying, 'What will we eat?' or 'What will we drink?' or 'What will we wear for clothing?' ³² For the Gentiles eagerly seek all these things; for your heavenly Father knows that you need all these things. ³³ But seek first His kingdom and His righteousness, and all these things will be added to you. **~Matthew 6:31-33**

⁶ Therefore humble yourselves under the mighty hand of God, that He may exalt you at the proper time, ⁷ casting all your anxiety on Him, because He cares for you.
~1 Peter 5:6-7

[33] These things I have spoken to you, so that in Me you may have peace. In the world you have tribulation, but take courage; I have overcome the world." ~**John 16:33**

Lord, I know that worrying does not accomplish anything. Help me to know how destructive stress and worry are and help me to learn how to counter worry with faith in You. I need to remember that worry is the opposite of trusting You and instead of worrying I need to use that energy in prayer.

Jesus, help me to redirect my attention, to focus on you instead of my stressful situation, my worry. Help me to build faith so that I know that You will always take care of me because You care about me. Help me to find courage and peace in You because You have overcome the world.

[10] Create in me a clean heart, O God,
And renew a steadfast spirit within me. ~**Psalm 51:10**

[1] Be gracious to me, O God, be gracious to me,
For my soul takes refuge in You;
And in the shadow of Your wings I will take refuge
Until destruction passes by. ~**Psalm 57:1**

Praying God's Word

against Fear

[13] I can do all things through Him who strengthens me.
~Philippians 4:13

[7] For God has not given us a spirit of timidity, but of power and love and discipline. **~2 Timothy 1:7**

[1] God is our refuge and strength,
A very present help in trouble. **~Psalm 46:1**

[6] Be strong and courageous, do not be afraid or tremble at them, for the LORD your God is the one who goes with you. He will not fail you or forsake you.
~Deuteronomy 31:6

Lord, I can do all things through you who strengthen me. You said that I should fear no evil; You did not give me a spirit of fear or timidity, but of power and love and discipline.

Let me rest in You as you are my refuge and strength. Give me a heart that is strong and courageous and help me to always remember that You will NEVER fail me nor forsake me; I put my trust in you.

[4] Even though I walk through the valley of the shadow of death, I fear no evil, for You are with me;
Your rod and Your staff, they comfort me. **~Psalm 23:4**

[1] The LORD is my light and my salvation; Whom shall I fear? The LORD is the defense of my life;
Whom shall I dread? **~Psalm 27-1**

[3] When I am afraid,
I will put my trust in You.
[4] In God, whose word I praise,
In God I have put my trust;
I shall not be afraid.
What can *mere* man do to me?
[5] All day long they distort my words;
All their thoughts are against me for evil.
[6] They attack, they lurk,
They watch my steps,
As they have waited *to take* my life.
[7] Because of wickedness, cast them forth,
In anger put down the peoples, O God!

[8] You have taken account of my wanderings;
Put my tears in Your bottle.
Are *they* not in Your book?
[9] Then my enemies will turn back in the day when I call;
This I know, that God is for me.
[10] In God, *whose* word I praise,
In the LORD, *whose* word I praise,
[11] In God I have put my trust, I shall not be afraid.
What can man do to me? ~**Psalm 56:3-11**

[1] The LORD is my light and my salvation;
Whom shall I fear?
The LORD is the defense of my life;
Whom shall I dread? ~**Psalm 27:1**

Praying God's Word

against Envy, Jealousy, Bitterness and an

Unforgiving Spirit

STEPHANIE A. MAYBERRY

[14] But if you have bitter jealousy and selfish ambition in your heart, do not be arrogant and so lie against the truth. [15] This wisdom is not that which comes down from above, but is earthly, natural, demonic. **~James 3:14-15**

[4] Love is patient, love is kind and is not jealous; love does not brag and is not arrogant, [5] does not act unbecomingly; it does not seek its own, is not provoked, does not take into account a wrong suffered, **~1 Corinthians 13:4-5**

[31] Let all bitterness and wrath and anger and clamor and slander be put away from you, along with all malice. [32] Be kind to one another, tender-hearted, forgiving each other, just as God in Christ also has forgiven you.
~Ephesians 4:31-32

[7] and in them you also once walked, when you were living in them. [8] But now you also, put them all aside: anger, wrath, malice, slander, and abusive speech from your mouth. **~Colossians 3:7-8**

[14] For if you forgive others for their transgressions, your heavenly Father will also forgive you. [15] But if you do not forgive others, then your Father will not forgive your transgressions. **~Matthew 6:14-15**

[19] Never take your own revenge, beloved, but leave room for the wrath of God, for it is written, "VENGEANCE IS MINE, I WILL REPAY," says the Lord. **~Romans 12:19**

[14] Bless those who persecute you; bless and do not curse. ~**Romans 12:14**

Lord, I want to have a right attitude, but sometimes it isn't very easy. I don't want to have envy, jealousy, bitterness or an unforgiving spirit, but sometimes my flesh rises up. Please give me the strength to conquer my flesh.

I want to have love for people, all people, the kind of love You have for everyone. I want to love people with a love that is patient, kind, not jealous, that does not take into account a wrong suffered. Help me to put away all my bitterness, wrath, anger, clamor, slander and malice, instead being tenderhearted and forgiving to others.

It is hard to forgive sometimes, Lord, but if I don't forgive others you won't forgive me. Help me to forgive others the way you forgive me, never taking revenge, but leaving it all up to you.

Give me a heart to love and bless those who persecute me, who treat me unkindly. Kill off the parts of me that offend You, Lord and fill me with You.

Praying God's Word

against Temptation

¹³ No temptation has overtaken you but such as is common to man; and God is faithful, who will not allow you to be tempted beyond what you are able, but with the temptation will provide the way of escape also, so that you will be able to endure it. ¹⁴ Therefore, my beloved, flee from idolatry. **~1 Corinthians 10:13-14**

¹⁴ But each one is tempted when he is carried away and enticed by his own lust. **~James 1:14**

¹² For the word of God is living and active and sharper than any two-edged sword, and piercing as far as the division of soul and spirit, of both joints and marrow, and able to judge the thoughts and intentions of the heart. **~Hebrews 4:12**

⁴ for the weapons of our warfare are not of the flesh, but divinely powerful for the destruction of fortresses. ⁵ *We are* destroying speculations and every lofty thing raised up against the knowledge of God, and *we are* taking every thought captive to the obedience of Christ, **~2 Corinthians 10:4-5**

¹⁸ Flee immorality. Every *other* sin that a man commits is outside the body, but the immoral man sins against his own body. **~1 Corinthians 6:18**

²² Now flee from youthful lusts and pursue righteousness, faith, love *and* peace, with those who call on the Lord from a pure heart. **~2 Timothy 2:22**

Jesus, you are faithful and your Word says that you will not allow me to be tempted beyond what I am able to resist and that you will provide a way to escape. But it is hard sometimes. Help me to resist temptation.

Your word is sharper than a two edge sword. Show me how to use Your Word to fight against temptation, against every sin, to flee immorality. Help me to pursue righteousness, faith, love and peace with You and make my heart pure.

[13]*"and do not lead us into temptation, but deliver us from evil. [For Yours is the kingdom and the power and the glory forever. Amen.']* ~**Matthew 6:13**

Praying God's Word

against Loneliness

35 Who will separate us from the love of Christ? Will tribulation, or distress, or persecution, or famine, or nakedness, or peril, or sword? **~Romans 8:35**

5 No man will *be able to* stand before you all the days of your life. Just as I have been with Moses, I will be with you; I will not fail you or forsake you. **~Joshua 1:5**

10 For my father and my mother have forsaken me,
But the LORD will take me up. **~Psalm 27:10**

15 Behold, I am with you and will keep you wherever you go, and will bring you back to this land; for I will not leave you until I have done what I have promised you
~Genesis 28:15

18 "I will not leave you as orphans; I will come to you
~John 14:18

24 A man of too many friends comes to ruin,
 But there is a friend who sticks closer than a brother.
~Proverbs 18:24

Jesus, I know that nothing can separate me from Your love, but I feel so alone! Let me feel You here with me. You said that You would never fail me, you will not leave me nor forsake me.

Your Word says that You stick closer than a brother, Jesus, and I really need a friend right now. People will let me down, but You said that You never will. I need to feel You now.

[37] But in all these things we overwhelmingly conquer through Him who loved us. [38] For I am convinced that neither death, nor life, nor angels, nor principalities, nor things present, nor things to come, nor powers, [39] nor height, nor depth, nor any other created thing, will be able to separate us from the love of God, which is in Christ Jesus our Lord. **~Romans 8:37-39**

My soul, wait in silence for God only,
For my hope is from Him. **~Psalm 62:5**

Praying God's Word

against Depression

¹³ A joyful heart makes a cheerful face,
But when the heart is sad, the spirit is broken.
~Proverbs 15:13

²² A joyful heart is good medicine,
But a broken spirit dries up the bones. **~Proverbs 17:22**

²⁸ Come to Me, all who are weary and heavy-laden, and I will give you rest. **~Matthew 11:28**

⁹ The LORD also will be a stronghold for the oppressed,
A stronghold in times of trouble; **~Psalm 9:9**

³ But You, O LORD, are a shield about me,
My glory and the One who lifts my head. **~Psalm 3:3**

Lord, I need You right now. I can't find happiness. I am so depressed; my heart is sad and my spirit is broken. I want a joyful heart, Lord! You said that when I am weary and heavy laden that you would give me rest. I need rest now, Jesus. You are my stronghold, my strength and my shield. I need you now. I need to feel you with me. Fill me with your spirit so that this depression will lift. Give me a joyful heart, Lord, and lift this depression from me. Give me a new heart.

⁷ Answer me quickly, O LORD, my spirit fails;
Do not hide Your face from me,

Or I will become like those who go down to the pit.

[8] Let me hear Your loving kindness in the morning;

For I trust in You;

Teach me the way in which I should walk;

For to You I lift up my soul. ~**Psalm 143:7-8**

[1] Hear my prayer, O LORD!

And let my cry for help come to You.

[2] Do not hide Your face from me in the day of my distress;

Incline Your ear to me;

In the day when I call answer me quickly.

[3] For my days have been consumed in smoke,

And my bones have been scorched like a hearth.

[4] My heart has been smitten like grass and has withered away,

Indeed, I forget to eat my bread.

[5] Because of the loudness of my groaning

My bones cling to my flesh.

[6] I resemble a pelican of the wilderness;

I have become like an owl of the waste places.

[7] I lie awake,

I have become like a lonely bird on a housetop.

[8] My enemies have reproached me all day long;

Those who deride me have used my *name* as a curse.

[9] For I have eaten ashes like bread

And mingled my drink with weeping

[10] Because of Your indignation and Your wrath,

For You have lifted me up and cast me away.

[11] My days are like a lengthened shadow,

And I wither away like grass. ~**Psalm 102:1-11**

Praying God's Word

for your Church

² And He was saying to them, "The harvest is plentiful, but the laborers are few; therefore beseech the Lord of the harvest to send out laborers into His harvest. **~Luke 10:2**

²⁰ And they went out and preached everywhere, while the Lord worked with them, and confirmed the word by the signs that followed. **~Mark 16:20**

²⁴ and let us consider how to stimulate one another to love and good deeds, ²⁵ not forsaking our own assembling together, as is the habit of some, but encouraging *one another*; and all the more as you see the day drawing near.
~Hebrews 10:24-25

¹ My brethren, do not hold your faith in our glorious Lord Jesus Christ with an attitude of personal favoritism. ² For if a man comes into your assembly with a gold ring and dressed in fine clothes, and there also comes in a poor man in dirty clothes, ³ and you pay special attention to the one who is wearing the fine clothes, and say, "You sit here in a good place," and you say to the poor man, "You stand over there, or sit down by my footstool," ⁴ have you not made distinctions among yourselves, and become judges with evil motives? **~James 2:1-4**

¹ Therefore I, the prisoner of the Lord, implore you to walk in a manner worthy of the calling with which you have been called, ² with all humility and gentleness, with patience, showing tolerance for one another in love, ³ being diligent to preserve the unity of the Spirit in the bond of

peace. [4] There is one body and one Spirit, just as also you were called in one hope of your calling; [5] one Lord, one faith, one baptism, [6] one God and Father of all who is over all and through all and in all. **~Ephesians 4:1-6**

Lord, I pray for my church. Give us all, the body as a whole, a heart to be laborers for You. Let us know that harvest as we reach out to souls and help people come to know You.

Give us a heart for stimulating each other to love and to do good deeds, encouraging each other as we come together in unity.

Let us not show favoritism, but welcome everyone who walks through those doors and has a sincere desire to know You. Let us not leave anyone alone or unattended.

Give us a heart for unity, for walking in one body, one spirit, tolerant of each other, gentle and humble, united in one God, one faith, one baptism.

Praying God's Word

for your Pastor (and his family)

¹⁷ The elders who rule well are to be considered worthy of double honor, especially those who work hard at preaching and teaching. **~1 Timothy 5:17**

¹² But we request of you, brethren, that you appreciate those who diligently labor among you, and have charge over you in the Lord and give you instruction, ¹³ and that you esteem them very highly in love because of their work. Live in peace with one another.
~1 Thessalonians 5:12-13

¹⁴ So also the Lord directed those who proclaim the gospel to get their living from the gospel. **~1 Corinthians 9:14**

¹⁰ Have You not made a hedge about him and his house and all that he has, on every side? You have blessed the work of his hands, and his possessions have increased in the land. **~Job 1:10**

² All these blessings will come upon you and overtake you if you obey the LORD your God: **~Deuteronomy 28:2**

¹⁶ that He would grant you, according to the riches of His glory, to be strengthened with power through His Spirit in the inner man, **~Ephesians 3:16**

² to malign no one, to be peaceable, gentle, showing every consideration for all men **~Titus 3:2**

Lord, I thank you for my pastor and his family. I appreciate them and I thank You for calling them to Your service. Give them double honor and place Your hedge of protection around my pastor, his family and his house. Let no evil touch them: keep them safe. Give them an abundance of blessings and give them favor.

Lord, give my pastor and his family strength to lead us, the body, and give them gentleness and a soft heart when dealing with people who may be unkind. Give them health and happiness and financial blessings. Dispatch angels to gather round about them, strengthening them, protecting them and uplifting them in all they do. Thank you, Jesus for my pastor and his family.

17 *The righteous* cry, and the LORD hears
And delivers them out of all their troubles.
18 The LORD is near to the brokenhearted
And saves those who are crushed in spirit.
19 Many are the afflictions of the righteous,
But the LORD delivers him out of them all.
~Psalm 34:17-19

5 Trust in the LORD with all your heart
And do not lean on your own understanding.
6 In all your ways acknowledge Him,
And He will make your paths straight. **~Proverbs 3:5-6**

11 For I know the plans that I have for you,' declares the LORD, 'plans for welfare and not for calamity to give you a future and a hope. **~Jeremiah 29:11**

26 My flesh and my heart may fail,
But God is the strength of my heart and my portion forever. **~Psalm 73:26**

Lord, it feels as if my heart is in pieces. You said that when we cry out that You will hear and deliver us from our troubles. You said that You are near to the brokenhearted and those who have a crushed spirit. I need to feel You with me now, Jesus. I need You to deliver me.

I need to feel Your comfort all around me. I trust You, Lord, with all my heart. I know that if I lean on You and acknowledge You in everything I do that You will make my path straight. I know that You have a plan for me that is for my welfare and good. You are my strength and my portion and I put my trust in You forever.

[11] You, O LORD, will not withhold Your compassion from me;
Your lovingkindness and Your truth will continually preserve me.
[12] For evils beyond number have surrounded me;
My iniquities have overtaken me, so that I am not able to see;
They are more numerous than the hairs of my head,
And my heart has failed me.
[13] Be pleased, O LORD, to deliver me;
Make haste, O LORD, to help me. **~Psalm 40:11-13**

[1] Hear my cry, O God;
Give heed to my prayer.
[2] From the end of the earth I call to You when my heart is faint;
Lead me to the rock that is higher than I.
[3] For You have been a refuge for me,
A tower of strength against the enemy. **~Psalm 61:1-3**

Praying God's Word

against Life Pressures

STEPHANIE A. MAYBERRY

Praying God's Word

to Strengthen you at School and Work

STEPHANIE A. MAYBERRY

School

[31] Whether, then, you eat or drink or whatever you do, do all to the glory of God. **~1 Corinthians 10:31**

[12] Let no one look down on your youthfulness, but *rather* in speech, conduct, love, faith *and* purity, show yourself an example of those who believe. **~1 Timothy 4:12**

[8] See to it that no one takes you captive through philosophy and empty deception, according to the tradition of men, according to the elementary principles of the world, rather than according to Christ. **~Colossians 2:8**

Jesus, I want to do a good job in school. I want to give You glory in all that I do. Help me to always be an example to others, to show others Your face through my speech, conduct, love, faith and purity.

As I pursue my studies, Lord, don't allow my mind to be taken captive through philosophy and empty deception according to the tradition of men. Instead, let me always know Your truth and walk in Your truth and light.

Work

[3] Commit your works to the LORD
And your plans will be established. **~Proverbs 16:3**

[23] Whatever you do, do your work heartily, as for the Lord rather than for men, **~Colossians 3:23**

[10] Whatever your hand finds to do, do *it* with *all* your might; for there is no activity or planning or knowledge or wisdom in Sheol where you are going. **~Ecclesiastes 9:10**

Lord, I commit my work to You, please establish my plans. I will work, always, in all that I do, as for You, to honor You, rather than for men. And whatever job I am given, Lord, help me to do it with all my might. Guide me on my job as I work but also let me be a witness, to show those around me Your love and grace.

Praying God's Word

for Godly Relationships

[4] Love is patient, love is kind *and* is not jealous; love does not brag *and* is not arrogant, [5] does not act unbecomingly; it does not seek its own, is not provoked, does not take into account a wrong *suffered*, [6] does not rejoice in unrighteousness, but rejoices with the truth; [7] bears all things, believes all things, hopes all things, endures all things. **~1 Corinthians 13:4-7**

[18] Flee immorality. Every *other* sin that a man commits is outside the body, but the immoral man sins against his own body. **~1 Corinthians 6:18**

[10] For if either of them falls, the one will lift up his companion. But woe to the one who falls when there is not another to lift him up. **~Ecclesiastes 4:10**

[17] A friend loves at all times,
And a brother is born for adversity. **~Proverbs 17:17**

[20] He who walks with wise men will be wise,
But the companion of fools will suffer harm.
~Proverbs 13:20

[17] Iron sharpens iron,
So one man sharpens another. **~Proverbs 27:17**

[6] Faithful are the wounds of a friend,
But deceitful are the kisses of an enemy. **~Proverbs 27:6**

Lord, I want relationships that honor You. Help me to know the Christ-like love that You have for all of us. I want to show love that is patient, kind, not jealous or arrogant. I want a love in my heart for others that has the qualities that You desire for me to have.

Give me strength to resist temptation and things that would cause me to act immorally – a sin against my own body. Give me Godly friends, Jesus. Give me friends that will lift me up when I fall, who will be there for me, encourage me and help me.

And please make me a Godly friend to them, loving at all times. Let us be united against adversity. Please direct me to wise companions who love You and will help me enrich my relationship with You. And please, Lord, help me avoid those you call fools, unbelievers.

Please make me wise in my friend choices: friends who can sharpen me and I them, friends who are faithful and honest to me. And help me to be that kind of friend to them.

Praying God's Word

for when you are under Spiritual Attack

⁸ Be of sober *spirit*, be on the alert. Your adversary, the devil, prowls around like a roaring lion, seeking someone to devour. ⁹ But resist him, firm in *your* faith, knowing that the same experiences of suffering are being accomplished by your brethren who are in the world. **~1 Peter 5:8-9**

¹² For our struggle is not against flesh and blood, but against the rulers, against the powers, against the world forces of this darkness, against the spiritual *forces* of wickedness in the heavenly *places*. **~Ephesians 6:12**

³ For though we walk in the flesh, we do not war according to the flesh, ⁴ for the weapons of our warfare are not of the flesh, but divinely powerful for the destruction of fortresses. **~2 Corinthians 10:3-4**

¹¹ Put on the full armor of God, so that you will be able to stand firm against the schemes of the devil.
~Ephesians 6:11

¹⁴ Stand firm therefore, HAVING GIRDED YOUR LOINS WITH TRUTH, and HAVING PUT ON THE BREASTPLATE OF RIGHTEOUSNESS, ¹⁵ and having shod YOUR FEET WITH THE PREPARATION OF THE GOSPEL OF PEACE; ¹⁶ in addition to all, taking up the shield of faith with which you will be able to extinguish all the flaming arrows of the evil *one*. ¹⁷And take THE HELMET OF SALVATION, and the sword of the Spirit, which is the word of God. **~Ephesians 6:14-17**

[22] Do not fear them, for the LORD your God is the one fighting for you. ~**Deuteronomy 3:22**

Jesus, make me sober and alert so that I am aware when the enemy attacks. Help me to recognize that my battle is not against flesh and blood, but against spiritual forces. Because we walk in the flesh but do not war according to it, help me to be patient with others who don't have this understanding so that I don't fight the person, but the spirit behind them that is driving them.

I prepare myself for battle, Lord, with the belt of truth, the breastplate of righteousness, my feet with the preparation of the gospel of peace. I take up my shield of faith, my helmet of salvation and the sword of the Spirit, Your Word, God. Make me a strong and courageous warrior, fight with me, Lord so I will not fear my enemies.

[1] Blessed be the LORD, my rock,
Who trains my hands for war,
Ana my fingers for battle; ~**Psalm 144:1**

[4] I call upon the LORD, who is worthy to be praised, And I am saved from my enemies. ~**2 Samuel 22:4**

Praying God's Word

when faced with Hard Decisions

STEPHANIE A. MAYBERRY

[30] I can do nothing on My own initiative. As I hear, I judge; and My judgment is just, because I do not seek My own will, but the will of Him who sent Me. **~John 5:30**

[13] Retain the standard of sound words which you have heard from me, in the faith and love which are in Christ Jesus. **~2 Timothy 1:13**

. [11] Do not participate in the unfruitful deeds of darkness, but instead even expose them; [12] for it is disgraceful even to speak of the things which are done by them in secret. **~Ephesians 5:11-12**

[15] Therefore be careful how you walk, not as unwise men but as wise, [16] making the most of your time, because the days are evil. [17] So then do not be foolish, but understand what the will of the Lord is. **~Ephesians 5:15-17**

[7] Do not be deceived, God is not mocked; for whatever a man sows, this he will also reap. [8] For the one who sows to his own flesh will from the flesh reap corruption, but the one who sows to the Spirit will from the Spirit reap eternal life. [9] Let us not lose heart in doing good, for in due time we will reap if we do not grow weary. **~Galatians 6:7-9**

[25] If we live by the Spirit, let us also walk by the Spirit. **~Galatians 5:25**

[7] BLESSED ARE THOSE WHOSE LAWLESS DEEDS HAVE BEEN FORGIVEN, AND WHOSE SINS HAVE BEEN COVERED. **~Romans 4:7**

Lord, I have a tough decision to make. I want my judgment to be just, so I do not want to seek my own will, but Yours. Help me to hold on to sound words and stand solid in You.

Please help to keep me from being drawn into participating in unfruitful deeds of darkness. I want to walk as a wise person and make the most of my time. Please protect me from evil that will cause me to walk as an unwise person. Please help me to understand what is Your will.

I want to reap what is good, what is of You, Jesus. Please help me walk in truth and give me a sharp mind that will keep me from deceit. I don't want to sow from my flesh because I will reap corruption. Instead, I want to sow from the spirit so that I will reap from the spirit and have eternal life.

Please Jesus, let your Spirit guide me. I want to live by the Spirit and walk by the Spirit so that I will not err.

Please forgive me for my sins, cover them in your precious blood and wipe my slate clean. Give me a heart, Lord, that I will make wise choices and keep from sin.

Praying God's Word

to Seek His Will

²⁷ My sheep hear My voice, and I know them, and they follow Me; **~John 10:27**

¹⁶ All Scripture is inspired by God and profitable for teaching, for reproof, for correction, for training in righteousness; **~2 Timothy 3:16**

³³ But seek first His kingdom and His righteousness, and all these things will be added to you. **~Matthew 6:33**

³ Commit your works to the LORD
And your plans will be established. **~Proverbs 16:3**

⁵ Trust in the LORD with all your heart
And do not lean on your own understanding.
⁶ In all your ways acknowledge Him,
And He will make your paths straight. **~Proverbs 3:5-6**

¹⁸ in everything give thanks; for this is God's will for you in Christ Jesus. **~1 Thessalonians 5:18**

² And do not be conformed to this world, but be transformed by the renewing of your mind, so that you may prove what the will of God is, that which is good and acceptable and perfect. **~Romans 12:2**

Jesus, I want to know Your voice. When I know Your voice, I can do Your will. I know that the way to learn to know Your voice is to study Your Word. Lord, please open my mind and heart so that Your Word becomes ingrained in my spirit and permeates my heart. That way, I will know Your voice and can do Your will.

In all that I do, I will first seek Your kingdom and Your righteousness so that I may know Your will for me. Please make it apparent to me so that I may know it and please give me the right attitude to accept Your will for me always.

I commit all my works to You, Lord so that You may establish my plans. I trust in You with all my heart. I do not rely on my own understanding but acknowledge You in all my ways so that You will make my paths straight. I thank You for all that You do, for Your will for me.

I do not want to be conformed to the world, Jesus. Transform me by renewing my mind so that I can do Your good and acceptable and perfect will for me.

Praying God's Word

to Strengthen your Relationship with Him

STEPHANIE A. MAYBERRY

37 And He said to him, " 'YOU SHALL LOVE THE LORD YOUR GOD WITH ALL YOUR HEART, AND WITH ALL YOUR SOUL, AND WITH ALL YOUR MIND.' 38 This is the great and foremost commandment. **~Matthew 22:37-38**

3 "You shall have no other gods before Me. **~Exodus 20:3**

23 for all have sinned and fall short of the glory of God **~Romans 3:23**

9 If we confess our sins, He is faithful and righteous to forgive us our sins and to cleanse us from all unrighteousness. **~1 John 1:9**

19 Therefore repent and return, so that your sins may be wiped away, in order that times of refreshing may come from the presence of the Lord **~Acts 3:19**

17 pray without ceasing; **~1 Thessalonians 5:17**

31 So Jesus was saying to those Jews who had believed Him, "If you continue in My word, then you are truly disciples of Mine; 32 and you will know the truth, and the truth will make you free." **~John 8:31-32**

27 Peace I leave with you; My peace I give to you; not as the world gives do I give to you. Do not let your heart be troubled, nor let it be fearful. **~John 14:27**

Lord, I do love You with all my heart and all my soul and all my mind. There is no one above You in my life. Help me to keep Your commandments and always keep You first in my life as you commanded, putting You before my family, my friends, my romantic relationships, my school, my job, everything.

I am a sinner and I thank You for Your forgiveness. Please forgive me for my sins, those that I know and those that I do not know. Please heighten my awareness and give me knowledge and wisdom and discernment so that I can recognize my unknown sins and correct them.

I want a deeper, more meaningful relationship with You. Help me to learn how to pray without ceasing, giving You praise and glory, praying for others and praying for my own supplication.

You said that if I walk in Your Word then I will truly be a disciple of Yours, I will know the truth and Your truth will make me free. I want to be free! I want Your truth!

Help me to strengthen my faith in You so that my heart will not be troubled and I will not know fear. I thank You for the peace and joy You put in my heart. Draw me closer and closer so that I can come to know You more and more.

[38] Peter said to them, "Repent, and each of you be baptized in the name of Jesus Christ for the forgiveness of your sins; and you will receive the gift of the Holy Spirit. ~**Acts 2:38**

[4] And they were all filled with the Holy Spirit and began to speak with other tongues, as the Spirit was giving them utterance. ~**Acts 2:4**

[3] This is good and acceptable in the sight of God our Savior, [4] who desires all men to be saved and to come to the knowledge of the truth. ~**1 Timothy 2:3-4**

[9] However, you are not in the flesh but in the Spirit, if indeed the Spirit of God dwells in you. But if anyone does not have the Spirit of Christ, he does not belong to Him. ~**Romans 8:9**

[5] Jesus answered, "Truly, truly, I say to you, unless one is born of water and the Spirit he cannot enter into the kingdom of God. ~**John 3:5**

[9] "So I say to you, ask, and it will be given to you; seek, and you will find; knock, and it will be opened to you. [10] For everyone who asks, receives; and he who seeks, finds; and to him who knocks, it will be opened. [11] Now suppose one of you fathers is asked by his son for a fish; he will not give him a snake instead of a fish, will he? [12] Or if he is asked for an egg, he will not give him a scorpion, will he? [13] If you then, being evil, know how to give good gifts to your children, how much more will your heavenly Father give the Holy Spirit to those who ask Him?" ~**Luke 11:9-13**

¹⁷ Now the Lord is the Spirit, and where the Spirit of the Lord is, there is liberty. ~**2 Corinthians 3:17**

⁸ but you will receive power when the Holy Spirit has come upon you; and you shall be My witnesses both in Jerusalem, and in all Judea and Samaria, and even to the remotest part of the earth." ~**Acts 1:8**

¹² "I have many more things to say to you, but you cannot bear them now. ¹³ But when He, the Spirit of truth, comes, He will guide you into all the truth; for He will not speak on His own initiative, but whatever He hears, He will speak; and He will disclose to you what is to come. ¹⁴ He will glorify Me, for He will take of Mine and will disclose it to you. ~**John 16:7-14**

Lord, please forgive me for my sins (recognize any unrepented sin and ask for forgiveness). I want to be filled with Your Spirit and speak with other tongues. I know it is Your will that I be filled with the Holy Spirit because it is Your will that everyone be saved. I know that being filled with the Holy Spirit is necessary for my salvation because You said that anyone who does not have Your Spirit is not Yours and will not enter Your Kingdom. I want to enter Your Kingdom, Jesus.

You said You would give Your Spirit to whoever would ask You so I am asking you, Lord. I am asking you to fill me with Your Spirit, the Holy Spirit.

You said where Your Spirit is, there is Liberty, I want that liberty. You said those filled with Your Spirit will have power and understanding, that Your Truth will be revealed to me. I want that power and understanding, Jesus. I want to know Your Truth. I want You to glorify you and I want You revealed to me and in me.

Jesus, please fill me with Your Spirit, today, right now. I am asking, seeking, hungry for more of You. In Jesus name, fill me now.

NOTE: Keep asking and praying. I it is important that you pray this aloud. Raise your hands and pray. If you run out of words, just cry out, "Jesus! Jesus! Jesus!"

When you feel God moving on you, yield to Him. If your mouth is already engaged in prayer, it is an easy transition to praying in tongues as the Spirit give you utterance. When you feel the words in you, just let them flow – let God's Spirit flow.

Praying God's Word

to Praise Him

STEPHANIE A. MAYBERRY

¹ It is good to give thanks to the LORD
And to sing praises to Your name, O Most High;
~Psalm 92:1

¹⁵ Through Him then, let us continually offer up a sacrifice of praise to God, that is, the fruit of lips that give thanks to His name. **~Hebrews 13:15**

¹ O come, let us sing for joy to the LORD,
Let us shout joyfully to the rock of our salvation.
² Let us come before His presence with thanksgiving,
Let us shout joyfully to Him with psalms.
³ For the LORD is a great God
And a great King above all gods, **~Psalm 95:1-3**

¹ Sing to the LORD a new song;
Sing to the LORD, all the earth.
² Sing to the LORD, bless His name;
Proclaim good tidings of His salvation from day to day.
³ Tell of His glory among the nations,
His wonderful deeds among all the peoples.
⁴ For great is the LORD and greatly to be praised;
He is to be feared above all gods. **~Psalm 96:1-4**

Jesus, it is good to give thanks to You, to praise Your name. You are mighty, You are holy, You are most high. You are the beginning and the end, the alpha and omega. You are everything and I am nothing without You. I give thanks to You and bless Your holy name.

I will sing for joy to You, Jesus, shouting joyfully for You are the rock of my salvation. I come before Your presence with thanksgiving and shout joyfully to You with psalms. You are a great God, a great King above all gods.

I will sing You a new song, I will bless Your name. I will rejoice in the new life You have given me and proclaim the good tidings of Your salvation every day. I will glorify You to all the nations telling everyone Your wondrous ways. You are great, Lord and greatly to be praised. There is no one above you. I thank You, Jesus!

[1] I will give thanks to the LORD with all my heart;
I will tell of all Your wonders.
[2] I will be glad and exult in You;
I will sing praise to Your name, O Most High.

[3] When my enemies turn back,
They stumble and perish before You.
[4] For You have maintained my just cause;
You have sat on the throne judging righteously.
[5] You have rebuked the nations, You have destroyed the wicked;
You have blotted out their name forever and ever.
[6] The enemy has come to an end in perpetual ruins,
And You have uprooted the cities;

The very memory of them has perished.

7 But the LORD abides forever;
He has established His throne for judgment,
8 And He will judge the world in righteousness;
He will execute judgment for the peoples with equity.
9 The LORD also will be a stronghold for the oppressed,
A stronghold in times of trouble;
10 And those who know Your name will put their trust in
You,
For You, O LORD, have not forsaken those who seek
You.

11 Sing praises to the LORD, who dwells in Zion;
Declare among the peoples His deeds.
12 For He who requires blood remembers them;
He does not forget the cry of the afflicted.
13 Be gracious to me, O LORD;
See my affliction from those who hate me,
You who lift me up from the gates of death,
14 That I may tell of all Your praises,
That in the gates of the daughter of Zion
I may rejoice in Your salvation.
15 The nations have sunk down in the pit which they have
made;
In the net which they hid, their own foot has been caught.
16 The LORD has made Himself known;
He has executed judgment.
In the work of his own hands the wicked is snared.

Higgaion Selah.

¹⁷ The wicked will return to Sheol,

Even all the nations who forget God.

¹⁸ For the needy will not always be forgotten,

Nor the hope of the afflicted perish forever.

¹⁹ Arise, O LORD, do not let man prevail;

Let the nations be judged before You.

²⁰ Put them in fear, O LORD;

Let the nations know that they are but men.

Selah. ~**Psalm 9:1-20**

ABOUT THE AUTHOR

"I have fully submitted myself to God, presented myself as an empty, willing vessel for Him to use. And that is how He uses me. Writing is my ministry; it is my service to Jesus."
~Stephanie A. Mayberry

Stephanie A. Mayberry is a Christian author whose passion for writing has become her ministry. A member of Christ Center Church in Goose Creek, South Carolina, she has given her life to God and is realizing her calling of ministry through her writing.

As an adult with Asperger's Syndrome, she ministers to other Aspies (people with Asperger's Syndrome) through her blog, The Christian Aspie and several books she has written about being a Christian with Asperger's Syndrome. She also uses her experiences with domestic violence to reach out to people who have been through abuse and help them find healing through Jesus.

But God has also impressed upon her to write other titles as well. As she says, "God writes the words, I just hold the pen."

Upcoming projects include a new believer series "OK, Jesus, now What?" and several books:

Joy in Ashes – Stephanie's firsthand account of God's faithfulness and provision during an unspeakably difficult trial in her life.

Boots on the Ground - Tells the story of Stephanie's experiences working with FEMA in the aftermath of Hurricane Sandy which devastated parts of New York and surrounding areas in October 2012.

Stephanie is a full time freelance writer and portrait photographer living in Goose Creek, South Carolina with her infinitely patient husband, C.W and her very confident Chihuahua (they haven't told him he is a little guy) Sunny.

www.StephanieMayberry.com

READ OTHER BOOKS
BY STEPHANIE A. MAYBERRY AT

https://www.amazon.com/author/stephaniemayberry

http://www.smashwords.com/profile/view/StephanieMayberry

VISIT STEPHANIE'S BLOG AT:

http://TheChristianAspie.com

CONNECT WITH STEPHANIE

Email: stephanie@thechristianaspie.com

Twitter: http://twitter.com/fotojunkie

Facebook:
http://www.facebook.com/stephanie.a.mayberry

Like Stephanie's Facebook Author Page
http://www.facebook.com/authorstephaniemayberry